About the Author

A distinguished veteran of the UK Armed Forces, the author brings a wealth of knowledge and expertise to the field of cybersecurity, cementing their credibility as a trusted voice in the industry. With over two decades in Communications and IT, followed by a successful transition into cybersecurity, they are uniquely positioned to tackle the complexities of digital security. Their profound understanding of robust control mechanisms allows organizations to combat ever-evolving threats, making them not only a practitioner but also a keen observer of the intricate balance between technology and security.

Having worked independently and collaborated with prominent organizations, including local and central government departments in the UK, the author has cultivated a rich professional background that spans diverse settings and challenges. Their military experience instilled a discipline and strategic approach to problem-solving that is evident in their practical work within the cybersecurity realm. This blend of military rigor and industry-savvy equips them with the tools necessary to not only implement but also innovate cutting-edge security frameworks that are vital in today's digital environment.

Their journey as a writer began with a desire to demystify cybersecurity for wider audiences, inspired by the complexities and the critical importance of this field. With formal education in Information Technology and further studies in cybersecurity frameworks, the author's academic background strengthens their narrative, adding layers of depth and authority to their insights. They seek to illuminate critical topics while making complex concepts accessible through engaging storytelling, ensuring their readers leave with not just knowledge, but also the confidence to apply it.

Passionate about sharing experiences and knowledge, the author's writing style is marked by clarity and relatability, enabling readers from various backgrounds to connect with the material. They believe in the transformative power of education and consistently aim to bridge the gap between expert jargon and public understanding. Through this book and various speaking engagements, they strive to cultivate awareness about cybersecurity, not just as a professional obligation, but as a fundamental component of modern life.

Driven by a mission to elevate the conversation around cybersecurity, the author aspires to empower individuals and organizations alike. Their future goals include not only writing additional works that explore emerging technologies and cybersecurity threats but also engaging in more speaking and consulting opportunities that foster deeper discussions in the industry. Each endeavor is fueled by a commitment to ensuring that cybersecurity is recognized as a shared responsibility in our increasingly interconnected world.

Table of Contents

Chapter 1: Introduction to Cyber Security Frameworks

(2) - 1.2 Importance of Standards in Cyber Security

(3) - 1.3 Overview of Common Frameworks

Chapter 2: Fundamental Concepts in Cyber Security

Chapter 3: NIST Cybersecurity Framework

Chapter 4: ISO/IEC 27001: Information Security Management

Chapter 5: COBIT Framework for IT Governance

Chapter 6: CIS Critical Security Controls

Chapter 7: FAIR Model for Risk Management

Chapter 8: PCI DSS: Standards for Payment Security

Chapter 9: ENISA's Framework for Cybersecurity

Chapter 10: Integrative Approaches to Cyber Security

Chapter 11: Governance, Risk, and Compliance (GRC)

Chapter 12: Cyber Security Assessment and Auditing

Chapter 13: Case Studies of Framework Implementation

(1) - 13.1 Successful Framework Adoption in Corporations

(2) - 13.2 Lessons Learned from Framework Failures

(3) - 13.3 Emerging Trends and Future Outlook

Chapter 14: Future Trends in Cyber Security Frameworks

(1) - 14.1 Evolving Cyber Threat Landscape

(2) - 14.2 Advances in Cyber Security Technologies

(3) - 14.3 Impact of Emerging Regulations

Chapter 15: Conclusion and Best Practices

Chapter 1: Introduction to Cyber Security Frameworks

1.1 Understanding Cyber Security Frameworks

A cyber security framework is a structured approach that provides guidelines, best practices, and standards aimed at managing cybersecurity risks. Frameworks are essential for organizations to systematically assess their security posture, identify vulnerabilities, and implement effective security measures. They offer a roadmap that not only facilitates regulatory compliance but also fosters a culture of security within the organization. By defining clear roles, responsibilities, and processes, a cyber security framework helps organizations coordinate their efforts and resources towards strengthening their defenses, thereby minimizing the likelihood of cyber incidents.

Effective cyber security frameworks consist of several critical components that work together to enhance an organization's security landscape. These components typically include well-defined security policies, risk management processes, incident response protocols, and continuous monitoring strategies. Security policies establish the foundation for acceptable behaviors and procedures regarding data handling and network access. Risk management processes help organizations identify, assess, and prioritize risks, allowing them to allocate resources efficiently. Incident response protocols ensure that there is a systematic method for addressing and mitigating security breaches when they occur. Continuous monitoring strategies provide organizations with real-time insight into their security posture, allowing for quick detection and response to potential threats.

Moreover, the integration of industry-specific standards within these frameworks can enhance their effectiveness. For example, frameworks such as the NIST Cybersecurity Framework or ISO/IEC 27001 provide tailored guidance that can align with an organization's unique operational needs. This aligns security goals with overall business objectives and helps in maintaining the integrity and confidentiality of critical information. Cyber security frameworks not only enhance protection against threats but also facilitate clearer communication about security risks to stakeholders and foster greater trust among clients and partners. Embracing a cyber security framework is not just a technical necessity; it is a strategic imperative for organizations aiming to thrive in today's digital landscape.

1.2 Importance of Standards in Cyber Security

Standards play a crucial role in promoting uniformity and best practices in cyber security efforts. By establishing clear guidelines, they help organizations define what constitutes effective security measures. This uniformity allows for more streamlined communication among teams, making it easier to identify vulnerabilities and implement appropriate controls. Additionally, when organizations adhere to recognized standards, they benefit from a collective knowledge base that incorporates lessons learned from previous incidents. Standards like ISO/IEC 27001, NIST Cybersecurity Framework, and others serve as reference points that organizations can use to assess their security posture against globally recognized benchmarks, ensuring that their efforts are aligned with established best practices.

The relationship between standards and organizational resilience against cyber threats is significant. When an organization implements recognized standards, it is better equipped to respond to and recover from cyber incidents. These standards not only outline preventive measures but also provide a framework for incident response and recovery. The structured approach they offer ensures that organizations can quickly adapt to new threats, minimizing the potential impact on operations. By fostering a culture of proactive risk management and continuous improvement, standards enable organizations to maintain a robust security posture that can withstand evolving cyber threats.

For professionals looking to enhance their cyber security framework, it is essential to stay informed about the various standards available and how they can be effectively integrated into existing security strategies. Aligning with recognized standards not only strengthens security measures but also enhances stakeholder confidence in the organization's ability to manage cyber risks effectively. A practical tip is to regularly review and update your organization's compliance with these standards, ensuring that they reflect the latest threats and changes in the cyber landscape, thereby maintaining an effective security environment.

1.3 Overview of Common Frameworks

Cyber security frameworks serve as structured guidelines, enabling organizations to bolster their security posture and manage cyber risks effectively. Widely adopted frameworks, such as the NIST Cybersecurity Framework, ISO/IEC 27001, and the CIS Controls, provide organizations with essential principles, procedures, and best practices for securing their sensitive information and technological assets. These frameworks are dynamically designed to address the evolving nature of cyber threats by outlining systematic approaches for identifying, protecting against, detecting, responding to, and recovering from cyber incidents. The adoption of these frameworks creates a unified language and a common set of standards among professionals, facilitating consistent and effective communication within and across organizations.

Each framework has unique features that make it particularly suited for addressing specific security challenges. For instance, while the NIST framework is particularly robust in government and critical infrastructure contexts, ISO/IEC 27001 is recognized globally and provides a comprehensive approach to managing information security risks, making it suitable for diverse industries. Organizations facing compliance requirements with regulations like GDPR or HIPAA can leverage these frameworks to ensure they meet legal obligations while establishing effective risk management practices. Frameworks such as the CIS Controls provide actionable recommendations that are ideal for organizations starting their security journey or those looking to strengthen their existing security measures. Understanding how to leverage these frameworks signifies a critical step toward building resilient cyber security measures tailored to an organization's unique risk landscape.

For those in the cyber security profession, familiarizing oneself with these frameworks is crucial. Not only does it enhance an individual's knowledge and skill set, but it also aids in aligning security policies with business objectives. Regularly consulting these frameworks helps ensure that strategies evolve along with emerging threats. One practical tip is to periodically assess your organization's compliance with the selected framework, as this not only reinforces security measures but also improves the overall security culture within the organization.

Chapter 2: Fundamental Concepts in Cyber Security

2.1 Key Terminology in Cyber Security

Understanding essential terms in cyber security is vital for professionals operating in this ever-evolving field. The lexicon includes a range of concepts, such as threat, which refers to any potential danger that can exploit a vulnerability. Vulnerability is the weakness in a system that can be exploited by threats. Another crucial term is risk, which represents the potential of loss or damage when a threat exploits a vulnerability. Additionally, malware is a broad category of malicious software designed to disrupt, damage, or gain unauthorized access to systems. Familiarity with these terms enables professionals to navigate the complex discussions surrounding cyber security effectively.

Clear communication among cyber security professionals is significantly enhanced by a mutual understanding of common terminology. Using standardized terms helps prevent misunderstandings in discussions about threats, defenses, and incident responses. For instance, when a team can uniformly define what constitutes a data breach, they can collaborate more efficiently in developing strategies to prevent and respond to such incidents. Shared vocabulary also plays a critical role in training and education, allowing organizations to create a coherent understanding of security practices both internally and externally. Establishing a common lexicon not only fosters teamwork but also aids in the development of comprehensive policies and procedures that protect information assets.

Emphasizing the importance of common terminology is not merely a matter of convenience; it is foundational to effective cyber security frameworks and standards. Adopting a standardized language supports consistent implementation of security measures across various platforms and industries. This consistency, in turn, contributes to more secure environments, as teams are better equipped to identify and respond to emerging threats swiftly. A practical tip for professionals is to create a glossary of key terms within your organization, ensuring everyone is on the same page and able to communicate clearly about security issues.

2.2 Risk Management Principles

Core principles of risk management serve as the foundation for securing cyber assets effectively. Understanding these principles allows organizations to establish a robust framework to protect their digital resources from various threats. The first critical principle is the identification of assets, which involves recognizing all components of the information system that require protection. This includes hardware, software, data, and communications, all of which need to be assessed for their value to the organization. To comprehensively protect cyber assets, it's vital to understand the potential risks related to each asset, including vulnerabilities that could be exploited by malicious actors. The adequacy of existing controls must also be evaluated to determine if they can sufficiently protect against identified threats. Without this foundational knowledge, organizations may inadvertently leave critical vulnerabilities unaddressed.

Once the assets and their associated risks are identified, the next step is risk assessment. This process evaluates the likelihood of various risks and the potential impact they could have on the organization. Various methodologies can be used for this evaluation, including qualitative methods, which focus on the subjective judgment of risk, or quantitative methods that aim to measure risk in numerical terms.

After assessing risk, organizations should prioritize which risks to address based on the potential impact and likelihood of occurrence. Mitigation strategies can then be developed. These strategies may range from accepting the risk, implementing additional safeguards, or transferring the risk through insurance or outsourcing. It's essential to adapt and refine these strategies continuously, as the cyber threat landscape is always evolving.

In effectively mitigating risks, organizations should develop and implement a response plan, detailing the actions to be taken when a specific threat materializes. Training and awareness campaigns for employees can also greatly enhance the organization's risk posture by fostering a culture of proactive cybersecurity behavior. It's essential to regularly review and update risk management processes, as emerging technologies and business operations can introduce new risks. Engaging with frameworks such as NIST Cybersecurity Framework or ISO 27001 can guide organizations to adopt best practices in risk management. Keeping abreast of these evolving frameworks not only helps in maintaining compliance but also fosters a proactive approach to addressing potential vulnerabilities within the organization.

2.3 Compliance and Regulatory Considerations

Compliance with laws, regulations, and policies in cybersecurity is essential for protecting sensitive information and maintaining the trust of stakeholders. Organizations face numerous legal requirements that dictate how they must secure data and manage risks. Failure to comply can not only result in hefty fines and legal consequences but also lead to reputational damage that can be difficult to recover from. An effective compliance program goes beyond mere checkbox compliance; it fosters a culture of security within an organization and helps align cybersecurity strategies with overall business objectives. This alignment is critical as organizations navigate an increasingly complex digital landscape, where the threat of cyberattacks looms large. Regulations compel organizations to adopt proactive measures and ensure ongoing vigilance, reinforcing the idea that cybersecurity is not just a technical issue but a fundamental aspect of sound business practice.

Various regulatory frameworks impact cybersecurity practices and set the standard for compliance. The General Data Protection Regulation (GDPR) is one of the most significant frameworks in recent years, establishing strict guidelines for data protection and privacy for individuals in the European Union. Companies that handle personal data of EU citizens must ensure transparency in data handling and breach notification procedures. Similarly, the Health Insurance Portability and Accountability Act (HIPAA) outlines the requirements for protecting patient health information in the healthcare sector, mandating the implementation of safeguards to ensure data confidentiality and integrity. In the United States, the Federal Information Security Management Act (FISMA) governs information security across federal agencies and sets a benchmark for securing government data. Other frameworks, such as the Payment Card Industry Data Security Standard (PCI DSS), focus on securing payment card information. Understanding and adhering to these regulatory frameworks is paramount for organizations looking to establish robust cybersecurity practices while minimizing legal risks.

As regulatory landscapes continue to evolve, professionals must remain adaptable and informed. Continuous training and education are crucial in keeping cybersecurity teams aware of changes in laws and regulations that may impact their organizations. Investing in compliance is not only a legal obligation but a strategic advantage that can enhance an organization's resilience against cyber threats. A practical approach involves regularly reviewing and updating cybersecurity policies and procedures to comply with the latest regulations while integrating industry standards for best practices. This proactive stance will help organizations not only meet legal requirements but also build a framework that supports long-term security objectives.

Chapter 3: NIST Cybersecurity Framework

3.1 Structure and Components

The NIST Cybersecurity Framework comprises several core components that together establish a comprehensive model for organizations aiming to manage and reduce cybersecurity risks. At its foundational level, the framework is organized into five key functions: Identify, Protect, Detect, Respond, and Recover. Each function is designed to work synergistically, contributing to a holistic approach to cybersecurity. Within these functions, there are specific categories that group related activities, and these further break down into subcategories that detail specific outcomes and actions. This structured approach enables organizations to understand where they currently stand in their cybersecurity postures and identify areas for improvement through a detailed lens, aligning their security practices with business objectives and risk tolerance.

The structure of the NIST Cybersecurity Framework significantly aids organizations in managing cybersecurity risks by providing a clear roadmap for implementation and assessment. The layered approach allows organizations to assess their cybersecurity initiatives in a straightforward manner, allowing for quick identification of gaps in existing practices. By categorizing actions related to cybersecurity into the defined functions, organizations can easily prioritize their efforts and allocate resources where they are most needed. Furthermore, the flexibility of the framework assures that it can be tailored to fit the specific needs and complexities of different organizations, making it practical and effective across a diverse range of industries. The interplay between the functions, categories, and subcategories fosters a continuous cycle of improvement, encouraging organizations to regularly reassess their cyber posture and adapt to emerging threats.

Understanding the structure and components of the NIST Cybersecurity Framework not only enhances compliance but also promotes resilience in the face of evolving cyber threats. Organizations can derive significant value by continually updating their practices based on the framework's guidance, ensuring they remain vigilant in their cybersecurity efforts. A practical tip for organizations is to conduct regular assessments against the stated categories and subcategories, as this will help ensure that all aspects of the framework are being addressed, leading to a stronger and more holistic cybersecurity program.

3.2 Implementation Tiers and Profiles

The tiered approach within the cybersecurity framework categorizes organizational maturity into distinct levels that help organizations understand their current capabilities and areas needing improvement. These tiers range from partial to adaptive, guiding organizations through a systematic evaluation of their cybersecurity practices. A partial tier indicates ad hoc policies and practices, while an adaptive tier reflects an organization that regularly adapts its cybersecurity strategies based on emerging threats and ongoing assessments. This structured way of organizing cybersecurity maturity allows organizations to identify their starting point, measure progress, and allocate resources more effectively to enhance their overall security posture. Recognizing where they fall within these tiers enables organizations to adopt a proactive stance in managing cybersecurity risks rather than reacting to incidents as they arise.

Profiles within this framework are instrumental in enabling organizations to customize their approach to risk management based on unique operational contexts and threat landscapes. By developing profiles, organizations can align their cybersecurity practices with specific business drivers, regulatory requirements, and risk tolerances. This tailored approach allows for a more precise allocation of resources, ensuring that organizations are addressing their most significant vulnerabilities without overextending themselves in areas that may not pose an immediate threat. Furthermore, profiles encourage continuous improvement by allowing organizations to periodically revisit and adjust their cybersecurity strategies as their environments change. Adopting this flexible framework not only enhances resilience but also fosters a culture of security awareness throughout the organization.

One practical tip for utilizing the implementation tiers and profiles effectively is to conduct regular assessments that move beyond mere compliance checks. Instead, focus on creating a culture where every team member understands their role in the cybersecurity landscape. Encourage feedback from across the organization during these assessments to build a comprehensive view of vulnerabilities and establish a more robust cybersecurity framework aligned with actual operational needs.

3.3 Challenges and Benefits of NIST Framework

Organizations often encounter a variety of challenges when implementing the NIST Cybersecurity Framework. One of the primary hurdles is the lack of awareness and understanding of the framework among employees. When team members are not familiar with the concepts and principles of cybersecurity, it becomes difficult to foster a culture of security awareness. Additionally, organizations may struggle with integrating the framework into existing processes. This integration can require significant adjustments, which can be met with resistance from staff who are accustomed to their current workflows. Moreover, aligning the framework with regulatory requirements can pose challenges, especially in industries that have specific compliance mandates. As companies work to adapt the framework to their unique operational contexts, they may find it challenging to maintain a balance between compliance and effective cybersecurity practices. Resource constraints are another common issue; organizations with limited budgets may find it difficult to invest in necessary training, tools, and technologies that support the implementation of the NIST Framework.

Despite the obstacles, the benefits of successfully adopting the NIST Cybersecurity Framework are substantial. By following the framework, organizations can enhance their cybersecurity posture significantly, leading to improved risk management. The structured approach provided by the NIST Framework allows businesses to identify their unique security threats and vulnerabilities, enabling them to prioritize their defensive strategies effectively. This proactive stance not only safeguards sensitive data but also builds trust with customers and stakeholders. Successful implementation also encourages a culture of continuous improvement, where organizations regularly reassess and refine their security practices. Moreover, the framework facilitates better engagement with external partners and regulators, as it is widely recognized and accepted in various industries. This recognition can streamline compliance processes and foster collaboration on cybersecurity initiatives. Ultimately, embracing the NIST Cybersecurity Framework can lead to a more resilient organization that is better equipped to respond to emerging threats in an ever-evolving digital landscape.

To ensure successful adoption of the NIST Framework, consider developing a comprehensive communication strategy to improve awareness and understanding across all levels of the organization. Engaging employees through training sessions and workshops can transform perceived hurdles into opportunities for growth and collaboration, building a stronger security culture that empowers everyone to contribute to the organization's cybersecurity efforts.

Chapter 4: ISO/IEC 27001: Information Security Management

4.1 Overview of ISO/IEC 27001

ISO/IEC 27001 serves as a cornerstone in the landscape of information security management systems. This international standard provides a systematic approach to managing sensitive company information, ensuring its confidentiality, integrity, and availability. By establishing a robust framework, organizations can effectively identify risks and implement necessary controls to mitigate these risks. The standard outlines requirements for establishing, implementing, maintaining, and continually improving an information security management system (ISMS), offering a strategic method to prevent data breaches and reduce overall security risks. Organizations adopting ISO/IEC 27001 can confidently showcase their commitment to safeguarding their information assets, which ultimately enhances their reputation and trust with stakeholders, clients, and regulators.

Aligning ISO/IEC 27001 with strategic organizational goals is essential for fostering a culture of security within an enterprise. The adoption of this standard enables organizations to create a security framework that not only protects sensitive data but also aligns with key business objectives, such as regulatory compliance, operational resilience, and competitive advantage. By integrating security practices into the organization's strategic planning, businesses can operate more effectively and respond swiftly to emerging threats. Furthermore, ISO/IEC 27001 provides a clear methodology for assessing and improving security measures, enabling organizations to track their performance against objectives and continuously advance their security posture. In this way, the standard goes beyond mere compliance; it becomes a tool for driving organizational success and innovation in a rapidly evolving digital landscape.

Utilizing ISO/IEC 27001 can significantly enhance an organization's ability to protect itself against cyber threats. To maximize the benefits of this standard, businesses should ensure they engage all levels of the organization in their information security initiatives, fostering a collective sense of responsibility. Training and awareness programs about the importance of information security practices will empower employees and create a more secure work environment. Additionally, periodically reviewing and updating security measures in line with evolving threats is crucial. This proactive approach not only ensures compliance with ISO/IEC 27001 but also positions the organization as a leader in information security management.

4.2 Key Clauses and Annex A Controls

The essential clauses of ISO/IEC 27001 address the specific controls and requirements critical for establishing and maintaining an effective information security management system (ISMS). Central to these clauses is the commitment to protect the confidentiality, integrity, and availability of information. Clause 4 emphasizes the importance of context—understanding the organization, its stakeholders, and the external/internal factors that might affect its information security posture. This clause sets a foundation that guides the implementation of security controls tailored to any organization's unique circumstances.

As we delve deeper into the requirements, Clause 5 highlights the need for leadership and commitment from top management. Their active involvement is vital for ensuring that the ISMS is fully integrated into the organization's processes. Commitment from leadership often translates into a culture where information security is prioritized and infused into day-to-day operations. Additionally, Clause 6 focuses on planning, requiring organizations to assess risks and opportunities, enabling them to identify necessary controls that will help mitigate risks while maximizing security opportunities.

Annex A categorizes specific controls that provide practical guidance on implementing best practices in information security management. These controls are grouped into various domains, such as organizational aspects, human resources, asset management, and access control, each of which addresses specific threats and vulnerabilities. For instance, the access control domain dictates the need for proper permissions to ensure only authorized personnel can access sensitive information, thereby protecting against unauthorized access or data breaches. The implementation of these controls should not merely be seen as a compliance exercise but rather as an integral part of risk management strategies that directly contribute to the resilience and security of an organization.

Furthermore, the overall effectiveness of the controls laid out in Annex A relies heavily on their implementation and ongoing monitoring. Organizations are encouraged to adopt a continual improvement approach, regularly reviewing and refining their security measures based on emerging threats, technological advancements, and changes in the business environment. Establishing a feedback loop through audits, penetration testing, and user training can enhance the resilience of the ISMS. Always remember that it is not just about having controls in place but ensuring that they are actively managed and adapted over time to face the evolving landscape of information security risks.

4.3 Certification Process and Requirements

Organizations seeking ISO/IEC 27001 certification must follow a defined series of steps to ensure compliance with the standard's framework. The journey begins with a thorough gap analysis that assesses current information security management practices against the requirements of ISO/IEC 27001. This initial audit helps identify areas for improvement. Once gaps are recognized, organizations must develop an action plan to address these deficiencies. The next critical step is establishing an Information Security Management System (ISMS), which involves documenting policies, procedures, and responsibilities geared towards securing sensitive information. Training and raising awareness among staff about information security roles and responsibilities is essential during this phase. Following the establishment of the ISMS, organizations should carry out an internal audit to verify that all processes align with ISO standards and to ensure that security controls are effectively implemented. After addressing any deficiencies identified during the internal audit, an external audit by a certified body can be arranged. This third-party validation is crucial for obtaining the certification. It confirms that the ISMS meets all relevant requirements of the ISO/IEC 27001 standard.

Preparing for successful certification requires considerable resources and commitment. Organizations must allocate sufficient time and personnel to manage the certification process. Designating a project lead to oversee this initiative can significantly enhance its effectiveness. In addition, investing in training for staff on both the ISO standards and the specific information security policies implemented is vital. This training ensures that employees understand their roles in maintaining security measures and complying with ISO/IEC 27001. Further, organizations need to develop comprehensive documentation of their ISMS, as well as maintain clear communication with all stakeholders involved in the process. Utilizing templates and guidelines for policy and procedure documentation can streamline this preparation phase. Additionally, engaging with a consultant who specializes in ISO/IEC 27001 can bring valuable expertise, helping to navigate complexities and ensuring that nothing is overlooked during the certification journey.

Effective preparation not only increases the chances of successfully obtaining certification but also strengthens the overall information security posture of the organization. Regularly reviewing and updating the ISMS post-certification is crucial, as it helps maintain compliance and addresses the evolving threat landscape. Consider implementing continuous improvement processes, such as scheduled reviews and feedback mechanisms, to enhance security measures further. This proactive approach ensures that the organization remains resilient against emerging risks and is well-positioned for future audits.

Chapter 5: COBIT Framework for IT Governance

5.1 Introduction to COBIT

COBIT, which stands for Control Objectives for Information and Related Technologies, is a comprehensive framework that assists organizations in aligning their IT initiatives with broader business goals. The significance of COBIT lies in its structured approach to governance and management of enterprise information technology. As businesses navigate the digital landscape, the need to ensure that IT investments contribute to the overall strategy becomes paramount. COBIT provides principles, practices, and tools that help organizations ensure their IT systems are not only effective and efficient but also designed to mitigate risks. By implementing COBIT, organizations can enhance their decision-making processes, improve resource allocation, and ensure compliance across various regulatory requirements.

The adoption of COBIT in organizations is driven by several key factors. One major driver is the increasing complexity of IT environments and the need for robust governance to manage these complexities effectively. Organizations face constant cybersecurity threats and regulatory scrutiny, which necessitate a proactive approach to risk management. By utilizing COBIT, organizations can establish a common language for stakeholders, facilitating better communication and understanding around IT processes and goals. Furthermore, the growing emphasis on business agility means organizations must respond rapidly to changes in the market. COBIT provides a framework for continuous improvement, allowing businesses to adapt their IT strategies in alignment with shifting business landscapes. Those who integrate COBIT into their practices are better positioned to leverage technology as a strategic asset rather than just a support function.

As organizations consider implementing COBIT, it is beneficial to focus on the framework's alignment with specific business objectives. Prioritizing the integration of COBIT's principles can result in the establishment of clear performance metrics and accountability structures. This proactive stance not only addresses current cybersecurity challenges but also prepares organizations for future demands. Understanding the unique business context and tailoring COBIT to meet specific strategic goals can amplify its effectiveness. This approach can lead to improved operational outcomes, ensuring that IT continues to drive innovation and support organizational success.

5.2 Governance Objectives and Management Practices

Identifying the key governance objectives of COBIT in enhancing organizational governance is crucial for any professional aiming to improve their organization's control over information and information technology. COBIT, which stands for Control Objectives for Information and Related Technologies, focuses on aligning IT goals with business objectives. One fundamental governance objective is to ensure that IT investments support and create value for the organization. This means not only maximizing benefits but also managing risks effectively and optimizing resource utilization. Additionally, the framework emphasizes the importance of promoting accountability throughout the organization. With clear roles and responsibilities, COBIT helps mitigate the risks associated with technology management, ensuring decisions made regarding IT are transparent and traceable. Ultimately, these objectives help establish strong governance practices that lead to improved performance and a more resilient organization.

Management practices guided by the COBIT framework serve as a roadmap for organizations looking to enhance their IT governance. The COBIT framework provides a structured approach for the planning, implementation, and monitoring of governance processes. This encourages managers to adopt practices that facilitate continuous improvement. For instance, one key management practice is performance measurement. By establishing clear metrics and KPIs, organizations can assess how well their IT services are aligned with business goals and make informed decisions based on that data. Another vital practice is risk management, which involves identifying potential threats to information systems and implementing controls to mitigate those risks. These practices are not just about compliance; they foster a culture of proactive management and strategic alignment. When organizations incorporate these practices into their daily operations, they build a solid foundation for sustainable governance that enhances overall performance and drives business success.

Embracing the COBIT framework requires a commitment to continuous learning and adaptation. Organizations should foster an environment where employees at all levels understand the importance of governance in their roles. Regular training and updates on best practices will ensure that everyone is aligned with the organization's governance objectives. It is also valuable to keep an eye on how the market evolves and internationally recognized standards develop so that organizations can stay ahead of emerging threats and capitalize on new opportunities.

5.3 Integration with Other Frameworks

Integrating COBIT with other established frameworks such as ITIL (Information Technology Infrastructure Library) and NIST (National Institute of Standards and Technology) can significantly enhance governance in information technology. COBIT focuses primarily on governing and managing enterprise IT, providing a comprehensive framework for aligning IT with business goals. When integrated with ITIL, which aims at delivering quality IT services, organizations can create a balanced approach that not only enhances service management but also strengthens governance. For example, while ITIL provides best practices for service delivery, COBIT ensures that these services are aligned with broader business objectives, risk management, and compliance needs.

The NIST Cybersecurity Framework complements COBIT in a different way by providing guidelines designed to help organizations manage and reduce cybersecurity risk. By leveraging the NIST Framework's focus on identifying, protecting, detecting, responding, and recovering from cybersecurity incidents, organizations can ensure that their IT governance is resilient. Integrating these frameworks allows for a holistic view of governance that encompasses service delivery, cybersecurity, compliance, and overall business risk. Such integration not only increases efficiency but also fosters a culture of continuous improvement across the organization.

Real-world applications of integrated frameworks demonstrate the tangible benefits of this approach. Many organizations that have adopted a combination of COBIT, ITIL, and NIST have reported improved IT governance, enhanced collaboration among IT and business units, and increased agility in responding to changing regulatory requirements. For instance, a large financial institution utilized this integrated approach to streamline its compliance processes, resulting in fewer compliance breaches and a more robust risk management strategy. Similarly, a healthcare provider successfully combined ITIL's service management principles with COBIT's governance model to ensure that its IT systems not only met regulatory standards but also delivered high-quality patient care. Adopting an integrated framework not only aligns processes but also cultivates an environment where IT is seen as a strategic partner in achieving organizational objectives.

When considering the integration of multiple frameworks, it is essential to prioritize alignment between the frameworks' objectives and the organization's goals. Establishing clear communication channels among stakeholders throughout the integration process can significantly enhance the chances of success. By taking a collaborative approach, organizations can ensure that they are not only compliant but also strategically positioned to adapt to future challenges in IT governance.

Chapter 6: CIS Critical Security Controls

6.1 Overview of CIS Controls

The CIS Critical Security Controls serve as a comprehensive framework designed to help organizations manage and mitigate cybersecurity risks effectively. These controls are a set of best practices that provide clear guidance on the most crucial steps an organization should take to defend against the ever-evolving landscape of cyber threats. The primary objective of these controls is to prioritize and implement security measures that significantly reduce the likelihood and impact of potential cyber incidents. By aligning security efforts with the CIS Controls, organizations can effectively enhance their overall security posture and protect sensitive data from potential breaches.

A structured approach to security is essential for successfully navigating the complexities of today's digital environment. The CIS Controls introduce a tiered methodology that enables organizations to adopt a clear, actionable, and prioritized set of measures. This approach encapsulates 18 key controls, organized into three implementation groups that vary based on the maturity of an organization's security efforts. Such an organized framework allows security professionals to systematically assess their current capabilities, identify gaps, and establish a roadmap toward achieving a more resilient security practice. By following these structured guidelines, organizations can ensure they are not only complying with existing regulations but also proactively addressing emerging threats in the landscape.

Incorporating the CIS Critical Security Controls empowers organizations to build a security-first culture. It fosters awareness and encourages proactive behavior among employees, making them an integral part of the cybersecurity strategy. Adopting a framework like the CIS Controls not only helps mitigate risks but also supports incident response planning, compliance requirements, and ultimately builds a foundation for a more secure digital ecosystem. Regularly reviewing and updating these controls based on the latest threats and trends can further enhance an organization's defenses. To achieve maximum effectiveness, organizations should consider integrating the CIS Controls with other standards and frameworks like NIST or ISO, creating a robust security strategy tailored to their unique needs.

6.2 Implementation Groups and Best Practices

Implementation groups serve a vital role in organizing cybersecurity controls based on the specific capabilities of an organization. These groups help categorize and prioritize the implementation of controls by aligning them with the existing resources, risk profiles, and the overall cybersecurity maturity of the organization. Companies vary greatly in their technological infrastructure, workforce expertise, and operational experience, which means that a one-size-fits-all approach to cybersecurity is ineffective. By utilizing implementation groups, organizations can better assess their capabilities, thus allowing them to create a strategic plan for deploying the necessary controls in a practical manner that reflects their unique environment. This method not only aids in risk management but also enhances the overall operational efficiency by ensuring that organizations focus first on controls that align with their current state before progressing to more complex measures.

Successfully deploying the CIS Controls requires adherence to best practices that maximize their effectiveness. One key practice is ensuring thorough communication across departments. Cybersecurity is not solely the responsibility of the IT team; engaging stakeholders across the enterprise fosters a security-aware culture and promotes collective responsibility for cybersecurity initiatives. Regular training sessions should equip all employees with the knowledge needed to recognize threats and understand their role in the overall security structure. Additionally, continuous monitoring and assessment must be integrated into the deployment process. This means regularly revisiting the implemented controls, measuring their effectiveness, and making adjustments as necessary. Such iterative processes create resilience in the organization's cybersecurity posture and help in effectively responding to emerging threats and vulnerabilities.

Linking technical controls with clearly defined metrics can further enhance the deployment of the CIS Controls. By establishing quantifiable goals, organizations can track progress and make informed decisions on resource allocation and risk acceptance. Implementing a feedback loop allows teams to learn from incidents and improve future responses, reinforcing a cycle of continuous improvement. Another practical tip for effective deployment is to leverage external frameworks and benchmarks, which can provide additional context and guidance on achieving compliance and improving security measures. Roughly 70% of cybersecurity initiatives fail due to lack of executive support; aligning security objectives with business goals can increase stakeholder buy-in and allow for a more unified approach to cybersecurity.

6.3 Measuring Effectiveness of CIS Controls

Assessing the effectiveness of implemented CIS Controls requires structured methodologies that can clearly illustrate how well these security measures are protecting an organization. One widespread approach is the use of an assessment framework that aligns with the specific controls outlined within the CIS benchmarks. This involves evaluating the configuration and operational effectiveness of each control in place, assessing whether these controls are functioning as intended, and identifying any gaps that may exist. Regular audits and assessments can be integrated into this process, utilizing both automated tools and manual reviews. Additionally, the establishment of a baseline allows organizations to understand the normal operating environment, making it easier to spot discrepancies that may indicate control failures or malfunctions. These assessments often lead to actionable insights, helping organizations prioritize their security efforts based on risk and vulnerability exposure.

The importance of continuous improvement in evaluating the effectiveness of CIS Controls cannot be overstated. Cyber threats are constantly evolving, and a static approach to cybersecurity will inevitably lead to vulnerabilities. Regularly revisiting the established metrics and evaluation criteria ensures that security practices remain relevant and robust against new challenges. Key performance indicators (KPIs) can be established to measure the performance of CIS Controls over time. These metrics can include incident detection and response times, the frequency of successful audits, and user compliance levels. By continuously monitoring these metrics, organizations can gauge the effectiveness of their controls, enabling proactive adjustments to their security posture. This commitment to continuous improvement facilitates a culture of resilience, where security measures evolve alongside emerging threats, ultimately strengthening the overall defense mechanism.

A useful practical tip for professionals in cybersecurity is to adopt a cyclical evaluation approach, emphasizing not just regular assessments but also feedback loops that incorporate lessons learned into future practices. This could mean updating training for personnel based on recent incidents or refining policies based on audit findings. Engaging all stakeholders, from technical teams to executive leadership, can foster a comprehensive understanding of security needs and vulnerabilities, enhancing the adoption and effectiveness of CIS Controls across the organization.

Chapter 7: FAIR Model for Risk Management

7.1 Understanding the FAIR Framework

The FAIR (Factor Analysis of Information Risk) model offers a robust quantitative approach to risk management that is particularly suited for cybersecurity professionals. It transforms the qualitative aspects of risk into a quantifiable measure, allowing organizations to make informed decisions based on statistical data. By utilizing the FAIR model, organizations can conduct a rigorous analysis of their risks, measuring not just the potential impact of security events but also the likelihood of occurrence. This transforms seemingly abstract concepts into clear numerical values, facilitating better communication among stakeholders and enabling more effective resource allocation. The FAIR framework fosters a common ground for discussing risk within an organization, creating a language that resonates with both technical and non-technical participants alike.

Within the context of the FAIR framework, two key concepts play a crucial role: loss event frequency and loss magnitude. Loss event frequency refers to the estimated number of times a specific incident may occur within a set timeframe, often measured annually. This aspect of risk quantification emphasizes the probability of events happening rather than solely focusing on historical incidents. On the other hand, loss magnitude looks at the potential financial impact of a loss event, should it occur. This metric often encompasses direct costs as well as indirect implications, such as reputational damage or regulatory fines. By understanding how often losses might occur alongside their potential severity, organizations can prioritize their risk management strategies more effectively, ensuring they allocate resources to defend against the most significant threats they face.

Implementing the FAIR model requires a thorough understanding of both qualitative assessments and quantitative metrics. As cybersecurity professionals delve deeper into this framework, they will develop a more nuanced view of their organization's risk landscape. This depth of understanding not only aids in immediate operational decisions but also provides strategic insights that can shape long-term security posture. One practical approach for professionals is to begin with a pilot project that focuses on a specific risk scenario, allowing for a hands-on application of the FAIR principles while fostering a deeper organizational understanding of risk management.

7.2 Quantitative Risk Assessment Techniques

Within the FAIR framework, several techniques facilitate the execution of quantitative risk assessments. FAIR, which stands for Factor Analysis of Information Risk, offers a structured process designed to help professionals evaluate and communicate risk. One of the primary techniques is the utilization of data-driven models that quantify potential future losses due to security incidents. This framework emphasizes the importance of establishing a clear context for risk by identifying the assets at stake, the threats against them, and the vulnerabilities that could be exploited. By employing metrics such as loss expectancy, security incidents frequency, and effectiveness of existing controls, organizations can measure potential impacts more accurately. This emphasis on quantification adds clarity and rigor to the risk assessment process, enabling professionals to make informed decisions regarding risk management strategies.

In the application of metrics and models, the FAIR framework provides tools to measure potential impacts of identified risks systematically. This typically involves estimating both the probable frequency of adverse events and their financial consequences. For example, organizations can leverage historical data and predictive analytics to ascertain the likelihood of specific threats, adjusting their risk assessments based on emerging trends in cyber threats. Scenario analysis is also a key component, where different potential events are simulated to gauge how they might impact the organization financially. Such comprehensive evaluations help prioritize risks based on their potential impact, enabling organizations to allocate resources more effectively. The goal is to cultivate a proactive risk management approach, ensuring that cybersecurity measures not only respond to current threats but are also adaptable to future challenges.

Integrating quantitative risk assessment methodologies like those provided by the FAIR framework can significantly enhance an organization's security posture. By focusing on measurable and data-backed insights, professionals can advocate for necessary investments in cybersecurity measures. The ability to present risks in financial terms allows for discussions with stakeholders who may not have a technical background, ultimately leading to a more robust understanding of the importance of cybersecurity in the business context. As you consider implementing these techniques, remember to continuously refine your assessment models and metrics based on new data and emerging threats, fostering a culture of adaptive risk management that is responsive to today's fast-evolving cyber landscape.

7.3 Integrating FAIR with Other Frameworks

The FAIR framework, which focuses on quantifying risk in a structured manner, can seamlessly integrate with other existing cybersecurity frameworks such as NIST, ISO 27001, or CIS Controls. Each of these frameworks offers valuable guidelines and best practices for securing information systems, but they often stem from different philosophical approaches to risk and compliance. Integrating FAIR adds a quantitative dimension to these qualitative frameworks, allowing organizations to better assess and manage risks associated with their information assets. For instance, by embedding FAIR's risk assessment techniques within the NIST Cybersecurity Framework, a company can not only comply with regulatory requirements but also gain insightful metrics that drive decision-making processes and resource allocation. This integration effectively enhances the organization's overall risk management strategy, making it more robust and informed.

Combining quantitative risk assessment with qualitative frameworks achieves significant benefits for organizations striving for comprehensive cyber risk management. Quantitative assessments provide numeric values that highlight potential losses, probability of occurrence, and other critical metrics, allowing for precise comparisons and prioritization of risks. On the other hand, qualitative frameworks offer context, scenarios, and narrative-based insights that can be crucial for understanding the implications of those numbers in real-world situations. This blend allows organizations to turn abstract numbers into clear strategies and action plans. Moreover, it can foster better communication across various stakeholders—technical teams, management, and even external partners—by creating a shared language that bridges the gap between quantitative data and qualitative insights. Ultimately, the synergy created between FAIR and other frameworks leads to a more informed, adaptable, and responsive cybersecurity posture.

Organizations looking to adopt this integrative approach should evaluate their current frameworks and identify opportunities where the FAIR principles can enhance existing risk management practices. Encouraging collaboration between teams that traditionally use different methodologies can also foster a more holistic understanding of risk. Additionally, organizations can benefit from training programs that emphasize the interconnectivity of these frameworks, helping personnel appreciate both qualitative and quantitative perspectives in cybersecurity risk management. Understanding and leveraging these synergies are key to creating a resilient defense against the evolving landscape of cyber threats.

Chapter 8: PCI DSS: Standards for Payment Security

8.1 Overview of PCI DSS Requirements

The Payment Card Industry Data Security Standard (PCI DSS) is a comprehensive framework aimed at ensuring the secure handling of cardholder information by organizations that accept, process, store, or transmit credit card data. Established by major credit card companies, PCI DSS plays a crucial role in safeguarding sensitive payment data against breaches and fraud. This framework outlines best practices that organizations must adopt to enhance their security posture and protect customer payment information from unauthorized access. By adhering to these standards, businesses can foster trust and confidence among their clients, ultimately leading to a safer transactional environment in the digital marketplace.

Organizations seeking to comply with PCI DSS must navigate a set of key requirements designed to fortify their security measures. These include maintaining a secure network, implementing strong access control measures, regularly monitoring and testing networks, and ensuring the protection of cardholder data at all stages of its lifecycle. Specific mandates require companies to install and maintain a firewall to protect cardholder data, encrypt transmission of cardholder information across open and public networks, and restrict access to sensitive data on a "need-to-know" basis. Additionally, organizations must engage in regular vulnerability assessments and maintain a comprehensive security policy that addresses how to protect data and respond to security incidents. Each of these compliance requirements plays a pivotal role in creating a robust defense against potential threats and vulnerabilities in a constantly evolving cybersecurity landscape.

Understanding and implementing PCI DSS requirements is not merely about compliance; it's about recognizing the importance of protecting consumers and ensuring the integrity of payment systems. For professionals in the cybersecurity field, actively engaging with these standards can guide your organization's strategic planning and operational practices. It's advantageous to cultivate a culture of security awareness among staff and continually assess compliance status, adapting to new threats as they emerge. By prioritizing these security standards, organizations can significantly reduce their risk of data breaches and foster a safer payment ecosystem.

8.2 Self-Assessment and Compliance Steps

The self-assessment process for PCI compliance is an essential step for organizations that handle credit card transactions. This process enables businesses to evaluate their own security measures and identify any vulnerabilities that could potentially expose cardholder data. Organizations often begin by gathering relevant documentation related to their current security policies, procedures, and technologies in place. They should also perform a thorough review of the systems that store, process, or transmit cardholder data. Understanding the scope of the cardholder data environment is critical, as it allows organizations to focus their assessment on potential points of vulnerability. It is recommended that businesses utilize the PCI Self-Assessment Questionnaire (SAQ), which provides a structured approach to gauge compliance levels across various PCI Data Security Standards (DSS). By analyzing the responses and pinpointing areas requiring improvement, businesses can develop targeted remediation strategies that align with compliance expectations.

Achieving full compliance with PCI DSS requires a series of concrete steps that every organization should follow. First, it is vital to determine which version of the SAQ best fits the organization's business model and transaction volume. After prospective assessments, businesses should implement robust risk management practices that include regular security testing, maintaining secure networks, and ensuring access control measures are in place for all employees. Training staff on security awareness is another critical step, as often, human error is a major contributor to data breaches. Organizations should also ensure the installation and maintenance of efficient firewalls, along with regularly updating antivirus software. Additionally, they need to monitor and test networks, storing cardholder data securely, and maintaining an information security policy. Finally, documenting all processes and maintaining records of compliance activities is crucial, as these records serve as evidence of compliance in the event of an audit. Keeping an ongoing review and adherence to these practices will not only aid compliance but will also strengthen the overall security posture of the organization.

Implementing a continuous compliance monitoring program is a recommended practical approach. This practice not only helps maintain compliance once achieved but also fosters a culture of security within the organization, ensuring that all employees are engaged in protecting cardholder data every day.

8.3 Challenges in PCI Implementation

Implementing PCI DSS controls often presents numerous challenges for organizations, regardless of their size or sector. One of the primary difficulties is achieving a comprehensive understanding of the requirements, as the complexity of the standard can be overwhelming. Many organizations struggle to accurately assess their current security posture against PCI standards, leading to gaps in compliance that can expose them to risks. Additionally, aligning existing processes and systems with PCI requirements often necessitates significant changes, which can be resource-intensive and require substantial time and financial investment. Staff training and buy-in are also critical, as employees may resist changes or lack the necessary knowledge to support compliance processes. Furthermore, the evolving landscape of cyber threats requires organizations to remain vigilant and continuously adapt their security measures, creating additional pressure throughout the implementation phase.

To overcome these obstacles, organizations should adopt a structured approach to PCI compliance that emphasizes planning and integration. Conducting a thorough gap analysis can help organizations identify specific areas needing improvement, allowing them to prioritize their efforts effectively. Developing a comprehensive project plan that encompasses timelines, resource allocation, and roles can facilitate better coordination and execution of compliance initiatives. Investing in ongoing employee training ensures that staff members are well-informed about PCI requirements and recognize their roles in maintaining compliance. Additionally, leveraging external expertise, such as PCI compliance consultants or industry best practices, can provide valuable insights to expedite the implementation process. Continuous monitoring and regular audits can help organizations stay ahead of potential vulnerabilities and adjust their approaches as necessary, ensuring that they remain compliant and secure against emerging threats.

Regularly reviewing and updating compliance strategies is crucial for long-term success. Organizations should not view PCI compliance as a one-time project but rather as a continual process that evolves with shifts in technology and threat landscapes. Establishing a culture of security awareness among employees, fostering accountability, and encouraging ongoing education can significantly enhance compliance efforts. Emphasizing the importance of PCI compliance not only helps mitigate risks associated with data breaches but also reinforces trust with clients and stakeholders, positioning the organization as a responsible custodian of sensitive information.

Chapter 9: ENISA's Framework for Cybersecurity

9.1 Goals and Structure of ENISA Framework

The European Union Agency for Cybersecurity, commonly known as ENISA, plays a pivotal role in enhancing cybersecurity across Europe. Its primary objective is to promote a high level of cybersecurity by providing expert advice, fostering collaboration among EU member states, and supporting the implementation of cybersecurity policies. By developing an agile framework, ENISA aims to strengthen the resilience of the digital landscape against evolving threats. The agency emphasizes the importance of harmonizing security measures across countries to ensure a unified approach to cyber threats. This involves sharing best practices, conducting risk assessments, and offering training programs designed to elevate the cybersecurity skills of professionals and organizations alike. Through its efforts, ENISA not only raises awareness of cybersecurity challenges but also encourages proactive responses to mitigate risks and improve the overall security posture of EU nations.

The structure of the ENISA framework is designed to be comprehensive yet flexible, incorporating several core components that work in synergy to achieve its goals. At its foundation, the framework is built on collaboration among various stakeholders, including governments, private sector entities, and civil society. It includes a robust set of standards that guide the establishment of national cybersecurity strategies and initiatives. Such standards facilitate consistency across member states while allowing for adaptations based on local needs. Additionally, the framework is structured around essential pillars such as risk management, incident response, and cybersecurity awareness. Each pillar supports specific initiatives aimed at strengthening the capabilities of organizations to protect against, prepare for, and respond to cyber incidents. The structured approach ensures that ENISA can adapt to new challenges and technologies, optimizing the effectiveness of its programs in a rapidly evolving digital environment.

Ultimately, engaging with the ENISA framework provides invaluable guidance for cybersecurity professionals looking to align their practices with EU standards. By leveraging ENISA's resources, organizations can better prepare for emerging threats, improve their security measures, and contribute to the wider cybersecurity community. Adopting this framework not only enhances individual and organizational resilience but also promotes a collective effort towards a safer digital Europe.

9.2 Cyber Security Risk Management Focus

ENISA's approach to identifying and managing cybersecurity risks is vital in today's increasingly digital landscape. The European Union Agency for Cybersecurity emphasizes a comprehensive understanding of risk management principles tailored to the specific needs of organizations. This approach begins with a thorough assessment of assets, vulnerabilities, and potential threats, enabling organizations to create a clear picture of their risk environment. ENISA advocates for methods that involve both qualitative and quantitative assessments, allowing organizations to prioritize their risks effectively. Understanding the context of these risks—whether from a technical, organizational, or human perspective—strengthens an organization's overall security posture. The agency also promotes the use of frameworks, such as the NIST Cybersecurity Framework, which serves as a template for managing cybersecurity risks while ensuring compliance with EU regulations.

To aid organizations in their risk management endeavors, ENISA offers a range of tools and resources designed to streamline the risk assessment process. Among these tools is the Threat Landscape report, which provides insights into emerging threats and trends within the cybersecurity domain. Additionally, ENISA has developed risk assessment templates that guide organizations step-by-step through the risk evaluation process. These templates facilitate not only the identification of risks but also the development of effective mitigation strategies. Training and certification resources enhance the knowledge base of security professionals, equipping them with the skills necessary to implement these risk management practices. Furthermore, ENISA maintains a collaborative platform for sharing best practices among member states and the industry, ensuring that organizations can learn from each other and improve their security frameworks continually.

Staying informed about the latest cybersecurity threats and risk management techniques is crucial for any organization aiming to strengthen its defenses. Engaging with the resources and tools provided by ENISA can significantly enhance an organization's ability to anticipate, identify, and respond to cybersecurity challenges. As professionals work to implement these frameworks, they should remember that risk management is not a one-time effort but a continuous process of improvement and adaptation to new threats and changes within the organization.

9.3 Collaboration with Member States

ENISA, the European Union Agency for Cybersecurity, plays a pivotal role in fostering cooperation among EU member states to enhance cybersecurity. With the evolving landscape of cyber threats, it has become increasingly important for countries to work together. ENISA facilitates dialogue and collaboration through various initiatives and frameworks that encourage information sharing, joint exercises, and the development of best practices. By providing a platform for member states to connect, ENISA helps overcome barriers that may exist due to differing national policies or capabilities. This cooperative spirit is vital for elevating the cybersecurity posture across Europe, as cyber threats often transcend borders and require a unified response.

Several collaborative initiatives have been established under ENISA's guidance to strengthen the security framework across Europe. These include joint cybersecurity exercises and the creation of special task forces that focus on tackling specific threats. ENISA also supports the development of cybersecurity certifications, which help ensure a baseline security level across member states. Additionally, the agency has played a significant role in coordinating responses to incidents that may affect multiple countries, facilitating a faster and more effective reaction. Tools such as the European Cybersecurity Skills Framework have also been introduced, promoting workforce development and ensuring member states have the necessary skills to respond to cyber risks effectively.

Engaging with these collaborative efforts not only enhances national security but also contributes to the overall resilience of the EU's digital ecosystem. For professionals in the field, staying informed about ENISA's initiatives and actively participating in joint exercises can provide valuable insights and strengthen individual and organizational capabilities. Cybersecurity is a shared responsibility, and leveraging the resources and networks established by ENISA can lead to more robust defense mechanisms against evolving threats.

Chapter 10: Integrative Approaches to Cyber Security

10.1 Blending Multiple Frameworks

Incorporating principles from various security frameworks can lead to a more robust and comprehensive security approach. Each framework, whether it be NIST, ISO, or CIS, provides unique insights and methodologies tailored to different aspects of cybersecurity. By blending these frameworks, organizations can create a tailored strategy that not only addresses their specific needs but also enhances overall security posture. This hybrid approach allows for better risk management by leveraging the strengths of each framework, providing a holistic view of security risks, and ensuring that no critical area is overlooked. The essence of blending frameworks lies in combining best practices, controls, and metrics to achieve a well-rounded cybersecurity strategy that is adaptable and scalable as threats evolve.

However, there are distinct advantages and potential pitfalls to consider when blending frameworks in practice. On one hand, the advantages include the ability to fill gaps left by a single framework and the opportunity for continuous improvement as organizations can selectively implement controls that best meet their objectives. Additionally, using multiple frameworks can foster a culture of security that is integrated across various departments and stakeholder groups. On the other hand, the practice of blending frameworks can lead to confusion and inconsistencies if not managed properly. Organizations may inadvertently create overlaps in controls, which can result in wasted resources and added complexity. Furthermore, insufficient training on the combined frameworks can leave employees unsure of the established protocols, potentially leading to vulnerabilities.

To navigate these challenges, it is vital to establish a clear governance structure that outlines how the various frameworks will be integrated. Identify key personnel who are well-versed in each framework and can facilitate the blending process while maintaining effective communication across teams. Regular training and updates on the integrated framework will ensure that all stakeholders are aware of their roles and responsibilities, ultimately enhancing security effectiveness. Maintaining a flexible yet structured approach can provide organizations the agility they need to respond to evolving threats while maximizing the benefits of their blended security framework.

10.2 Frameworks in Different Industries

Different industries face unique challenges and risks when it comes to cyber security, leading them to adapt and implement various frameworks that cater to their specific needs. For instance, the financial sector, with its vast amounts of sensitive data and stringent regulatory requirements, often utilizes the NIST Cybersecurity Framework (NIST CSF) as a foundation for its security posture. This framework helps organizations in this sector to effectively identify, protect, detect, respond, and recover from cyber incidents. In contrast, the healthcare industry focuses on frameworks like HIPAA to safeguard patient information while ensuring compliance with privacy laws. These adaptations ensure that organizations not only meet compliance requirements but also enhance their overall security posture to mitigate risks effectively. As cyber threats evolve, organizations must regularly assess and customize their chosen frameworks to address emerging vulnerabilities while maximizing their operational capabilities.

Exploring case studies highlights how various sectors successfully implement cyber security frameworks to bolster their defenses. One notable example is a large retail corporation that adopted the PCI DSS (Payment Card Industry Data Security Standard) framework to secure customer payment information. This organization underwent substantial changes in its security practices, including the addition of encryption technologies and the establishment of a comprehensive security awareness training program for employees. As a result, this retailer significantly reduced data breaches and improved customer trust. Similarly, a manufacturing company faced with increasing threats in its operational technology environment turned to the ISA/IEC 62443 framework. By implementing this industrial cyber security standard, the organization successfully integrated security measures into its production processes, ensuring that its critical infrastructure remained operational while protecting against cyber threats. These examples demonstrate the effectiveness of tailored frameworks for addressing specific industry risks.

It is essential for professionals to recognize the importance of aligning cyber security frameworks with their industry's specific needs. By doing so, organizations can create a unique security posture that considers regulatory requirements, technology landscapes, and operational challenges. Continuous evaluation and adaptation not only help in maintaining compliance but also lead to a more resilient security infrastructure. Professionals should strive to stay updated on emerging frameworks and standards, as this knowledge will empower them to make informed decisions that enhance their organization's security efforts and ultimately contribute to a safer digital landscape.

10.3 Tailoring Frameworks to Organization Needs

Identifying methods for customizing cyber security frameworks to align with unique organizational contexts begins with a thorough understanding of the organization's structure, culture, and specific vulnerabilities. The frameworks such as NIST Cybersecurity Framework, ISO/IEC 27001, or CIS Controls offer a robust base, but their effectiveness hinges on how well they are customized to fit the organization's particular needs. Organizations must conduct a comprehensive risk assessment that not only identifies assets and threats but also gauges operational processes and human factors. This step informs the choice of controls and measures that best resonate with the organization's objectives and existing resources. Furthermore, stakeholder engagement is crucial; involving various departments can provide insights into operational risks that might not be apparent from a purely technical viewpoint. Adapting language, terminology, and emphasis within the framework to resonate with organizational culture ensures better buy-in and compliance across the board. Training resources tailored to staff at different levels also enhance understanding and implementation, reinforcing the importance of a tailored approach.

Highlighting strategies for continual alignment of frameworks with evolving business objectives is essential for maintaining a dynamic security posture. As businesses evolve, so too must their cyber security strategies. Implementing a regular review cycle is a foundational strategy; this should include assessing both internal business changes and external threats. Organizations should schedule periodic assessments, ideally quarterly, to revisit their cyber security frameworks, evaluating the efficacy of existing controls and identifying any gaps that have emerged due to shifts in business strategy or threat landscape. Continuous improvement can be reinforced by fostering a strong culture of communication from top-level management down through every department. Encouraging feedback and open discussions about the practicalities of the framework allows for ongoing adjustments and enhancements. Additionally, formalizing these discussions into documented reports can facilitate knowledge sharing and ensure that lessons learned feed back into the framework adjustments. By creating a flexible yet robust alignment process, organizations can adapt their cyber security frameworks consistently with their evolving business goals.

Organizations that integrate regular training sessions into their framework update processes can effectively empower their teams to adapt to changes swiftly. Providing employees with the tools and knowledge to understand not only what is changing but also why these changes are necessary can significantly enhance their commitment to the framework and its objectives.

Chapter 11: Governance, Risk, and Compliance (GRC)

11.1 Overview of GRC Concepts

Governance, risk, and compliance, often referred to collectively as GRC, are essential components in the landscape of cyber security. Governance involves the frameworks and processes that guide an organization's decisions and actions in a structured manner, ensuring alignment with its overall objectives. Risk, in the context of cyber security, pertains to the potential for loss or damage that can arise from threats exploiting vulnerabilities. Compliance involves adhering to laws, regulations, and standards that govern how organizations must operate, particularly in handling sensitive data and protecting digital assets. The critical interrelationships among these three elements cannot be overstated; effective governance sets the foundation for identifying and managing risks, while compliance requirements often shape governance frameworks and risk management practices. A well-integrated GRC approach aids organizations in understanding the complexities of their cyber environments while allowing them to better align their security initiatives with business goals and regulatory obligations.

The role of GRC in ensuring effective risk management and adherence to regulations is vital, especially in today's fast-evolving threat landscape. By adopting a GRC framework, organizations can systematically evaluate their risk exposure and implement strategies to mitigate those risks effectively. This structured approach enables businesses to prioritize security measures based not only on their specific risk profiles but also on regulatory requirements they must comply with. Additionally, GRC practices foster a culture of accountability and transparency across the organization, where stakeholders at all levels understand their responsibilities related to risk and compliance. By integrating GRC into daily operations, organizations are better equipped to respond to evolving threats and maintain continuous compliance with industry standards and government regulations, ultimately enhancing their resilience in the face of cyber challenges.

To strengthen your GRC efforts, regularly reviewing and updating your frameworks and processes is crucial. Keeping up with changes in regulations and emerging risks allows your organization to remain compliant while effectively managing potential cyber threats. This proactive stance not only helps in reducing vulnerabilities but also builds a solid foundation of trust with stakeholders, including customers and partners, who expect robust security measures in today's digital environment.

11.2 Role of GRC in Cyber Security Frameworks

GRC frameworks play a pivotal role in guiding organizations to establish robust cyber security practices. By integrating governance, risk management, and compliance into their security strategies, organizations can create a cohesive and comprehensive approach to managing cyber threats. GRC frameworks provide a structured methodology that enables organizations to identify vulnerabilities, assess risks, and implement necessary controls to protect sensitive information. Through these frameworks, organizations not only align their security initiatives with business objectives but also ensure that they are accountable to regulatory requirements and industry standards. This alignment helps in bridging the gap between IT security and business strategy, fostering a culture of security awareness throughout the organization.

Key GRC principles enhance the implementation of security frameworks in various ways. One crucial principle is that of continuous monitoring and assessment, which ensures that security controls are effective and adapted to the evolving threat landscape. Another essential principle is accountability, where clear roles and responsibilities are established, ensuring that everyone in the organization understands their part in promoting security. Additionally, a focus on risk management leads to informed decision-making when prioritizing security efforts. Organizations can also benefit from maintaining transparency in reporting to stakeholders, thereby reinforcing trust and demonstrating compliance. By embedding these principles into their cyber security practices, organizations can achieve a more resilient security posture while also minimizing vulnerabilities.

Integrating GRC into cyber security frameworks not only streamlines processes but also aids in cultivating a proactive security environment. For professionals looking to implement or enhance their security framework, considering how GRC principles align with their organizational goals will be instrumental. Regularly reviewing and updating GRC policies can lead to a more adaptable approach, allowing organizations to respond quickly to new threats while maintaining regulatory compliance. Developing a robust incident response plan that incorporates GRC principles can also considerably reduce the impact of potential security incidents, ensuring that organizations can recover and learn from such events effectively. Building a culture of security around GRC not only protects the organization's assets but also supports its overall strategic vision.

11.3 Tools and Technologies Supporting GRC

Technologies that facilitate Governance, Risk, and Compliance (GRC) management play a crucial role in enhancing security and aligning cybersecurity measures with organizational objectives. Modern GRC tools are equipped with features that allow businesses to assess risks, monitor compliance standards, and streamline reporting processes. These technologies include integrated risk management platforms, compliance management systems, and business continuity solutions that provide a comprehensive view of the organization's security posture. By employing these advanced tools, professionals can not only identify vulnerabilities but also ensure that proper controls are in place. Furthermore, data analytics within these systems helps organizations comprehend complex regulatory requirements and make informed decisions, ultimately fortifying their cybersecurity framework.

Automation emerges as a key enabler in achieving effective governance and ensuring compliance with industry standards. By automating routine compliance processes, companies can reduce manual errors and free their resources for more strategic tasks. For example, automated workflows can manage compliance audits and generate reports with minimal human intervention, ensuring accuracy and timeliness. This shift towards automation enhances visibility and accountability, as all actions are logged and can be reviewed easily during audits. Moreover, automation scales seamlessly with the organization, allowing businesses to adapt quickly to new regulations or changes in their operating environment without significant operational disruptions. The deployment of intelligent automation tools further aids in continuously monitoring security policies and compliance requirements, which ensures that organizations remain vigilant and proactive against cyber threats.

In the evolving landscape of cybersecurity and compliance, leveraging the right tools and technologies is not simply optional; it is essential for organizations striving to maintain a strong security posture. As professionals in the field, understanding how to effectively implement these technologies while embracing automation will empower organizations to navigate the complexities of GRC with greater confidence. It's vital to continually evaluate and refine the technologies at hand, ensuring they align not only with current needs but also with future challenges that may arise. Keeping abreast of emerging technologies and trends will provide a competitive edge in the fast-paced cybersecurity environment.

Chapter 12: Cyber Security Assessment and Auditing

12.1 Assessment Methodologies

Cybersecurity assessments are critical for identifying vulnerabilities, managing risks, and maintaining the integrity of information systems. Various methodologies exist, each tailored to different environments and purposes. One widely used approach is the Risk Assessment Methodology, which involves identifying, analyzing, and prioritizing risks to an organization's assets. This method allows professionals to quantify the potential impact of various threats and develop strategies to mitigate them effectively. Another prevalent methodology is the Compliance Assessment, often tied to regulatory frameworks like GDPR or HIPAA. This approach ensures that organizations meet specific legal requirements, helping to avoid costly penalties. The Security Maturity Model Assessment focuses on evaluating an organization's security posture against established best practices, fostering continuous improvement over time. Each of these methodologies offers distinct processes and tools designed to navigate the complex landscape of cybersecurity.

While these methodologies are effective, they come with their strengths and weaknesses. The Risk Assessment Methodology is comprehensive, providing detailed insights into potential threats. However, it can be resource-intensive and may require advanced expertise to execute properly. Conversely, Compliance Assessments are straightforward and target regulatory adherence, which is essential for many organizations. The downside is that they may overlook broader security risks that do not fall under specific compliance requirements. Maturity Model Assessments enable organizations to understand their security stance and prioritize improvements, though they can sometimes be perceived as overly prescriptive, leaving little room for flexibility based on unique organizational needs. Understanding these strengths and weaknesses is crucial in selecting the right assessment methodology that aligns with an organization's specific security goals.

As professionals embark on their cybersecurity assessment journey, integrating multiple methodologies can often yield the best outcomes. Combining elements of risk assessment with compliance checks can provide a balanced view of both security vulnerabilities and regulatory adherence. It is vital to tailor the chosen assessment methodology to the unique context and requirements of your organization while remaining agile enough to adapt to the evolving threat landscape. Staying updated on emerging trends and integrating feedback from assessments into practical security improvements can lead to a more resilient cybersecurity framework.

12.2 Continuous Monitoring Techniques

Maintaining an organization's cyber security posture requires a consistent and effective approach to ongoing monitoring. This involves continuously assessing and adapting the cyber security measures in place to respond adequately to evolving threats. Techniques for continual monitoring can include automated threat detection systems, which deploy algorithms to analyze network traffic in real-time. By implementing these systems, organizations can quickly identify unusual activity that may indicate a breach. Additionally, regular vulnerability assessments allow organizations to pinpoint weaknesses in their security infrastructure, helping teams prioritize and remediate issues before they become major problems. Integrating security information and event management (SIEM) systems is another critical technique, providing a centralized view of security data from various sources, enabling quicker response times to incidents.

To support the practice of continuous risk assessment and compliance, organizations should leverage a range of tools designed to provide visibility and accountability. Tools such as automated compliance checkers can ensure that regulatory standards are being met on an ongoing basis, reducing the risk of non-compliance penalties. Additionally, continuous integration/continuous delivery (CI/CD) tools in software development help ensure that security is embedded in the development process from the outset. Implementing regular audits of security policies and incident response plans allows organizations to remain agile and ready to respond to changing compliance requirements. These practices ensure that not only are risks identified and mitigated continuously, but that the organization has a sustainable posture that adapts to the dynamic nature of cyber threats.

Implementing these strategies effectively can lead to a strong security culture within an organization. Continuous monitoring encourages proactive behavior rather than reactive responses. Organizations can equip their teams with the knowledge that they are not just waiting for the next threat to appear but actively controlling their cyber security landscape. A practical tip is to combine automated tools with human oversight. While automation can help manage and analyze vast amounts of data quickly, human analysts possess the insight and critical thinking needed to understand the broader context of potential threats.

12.3 Audit Preparation and Best Practices

Preparing for a cybersecurity audit requires a strategic approach to ensure that organizations comply with industry standards and frameworks. Start by conducting a thorough assessment of existing cybersecurity policies, practices, and technologies. This assessment serves as the foundation for identifying gaps in compliance. Engage your team in understanding the specific framework or standard that the audit will be based on, whether it's NIST, ISO 27001, or another relevant guideline. Make sure everyone knows their roles in the preparation process, as collaboration fosters accountability. It's critical to gather and document evidence of compliance, which may include policies, incident response plans, training records, and system security configurations. Scheduling regular review meetings during the audit preparation phase can help maintain communication and ensure that everyone is aligned. It's also essential to identify and train internal team members who can act as liaisons during the audit, as their familiarity with the organization's operations will aid in addressing auditors' inquiries efficiently.

Managing an audit effectively requires careful planning and an organized approach. Develop a comprehensive timeline that encompasses all audit phases, from initial preparation to post-audit review. During the audit, maintain clear communication with auditors, providing them with necessary documentation and answering any questions promptly. This openness can facilitate a smoother audit process and build trust between your organization and the auditing team. After receiving audit results, analyze them thoroughly to identify areas for improvement. Create an actionable remediation plan that addresses any weaknesses or deficiencies highlighted in the audit. This plan should include concrete timelines and responsibilities to ensure that necessary changes are implemented. Reporting the findings to senior management can help emphasize the importance of continuous compliance and risk management. Regular audits, whether internal or external, should be part of a broader strategy to uphold a strong security posture, reinforcing the commitment to protecting sensitive information.

Consider implementing a continuous monitoring system that integrates with your existing cybersecurity framework. This proactive approach allows organizations to stay ahead of potential vulnerabilities and ensures that compliance measures are consistently upheld. Encourage a culture of security awareness among employees, as it plays a vital role in maintaining compliance long term. Use training programs to regularly update the team on new regulations and best practices. Involving employees in the audit process can also make them more aware of their individual responsibilities toward cybersecurity. Always remember that audits are not just a checklist but a valuable opportunity for improvement and growth in the organization's cybersecurity journey.

Chapter 13: Case Studies of Framework Implementation

13.1 Successful Framework Adoption in Corporations

Many organizations have successfully adopted cyber security frameworks, demonstrating the tangible benefits of a structured approach to security. One notable example is a major financial institution that implemented the NIST Cybersecurity Framework. Initially facing numerous data breaches, the organization adopted this framework to create a robust security posture. They conducted a thorough risk assessment, identified vulnerabilities, and tailored their security measures accordingly. This systematic approach allowed them to effectively manage threats, ultimately resulting in a significant reduction in incidents and enhanced customer trust.

Similarly, a healthcare provider embraced ISO/IEC 27001 to protect sensitive patient data. The organization knew that regulatory compliance was critical but also recognized a gap in understanding how to integrate these standards into their existing operations. They invested in training for their staff and created a culture of security awareness. This shift was pivotal; within a year, the organization not only achieved certification but also developed comprehensive protocols that improved incident response times. Patients felt more secure, and the provider could navigate compliance audits with greater confidence.

The retail sector showcases another compelling case. A large retail chain adopted the CIS Controls framework in response to several high-profile data breaches affecting the industry. By focusing on prioritized safeguards and implementing a continuous security improvement process, they effectively reduced their attack surface. The organization enhanced its monitoring capabilities and established clear guidelines for incident management. This proactive stance led to an observable decline in security incidents, while also fostering a heightened sense of accountability among employees, which is crucial in a sector where human error is a significant factor in security breaches.

Successful implementation of cyber security frameworks often hinges on several critical factors. Leadership commitment stands as perhaps the most significant. In all the organizations mentioned, executives prioritized security initiatives and allocated necessary resources. This commitment ensured that security was not just a checkbox but a core business objective, fostering an organizational culture that values safety and risk management.

Another essential factor is the engagement of employees at all levels. Organizations that effectively communicated the importance of the framework and involved their staff in the adoption process saw more significant buy-in. Training programs that emphasize the roles and responsibilities of all employees lead to greater awareness and vigilance, creating a unified front against potential threats.

Moreover, a well-defined implementation strategy simplifies the adoption process. Organizations that clearly outlined their goals, timelines, and milestones tended to stay focused and measure their progress effectively. This strategic coherence not only helps in maintaining momentum but also assists in troubleshooting issues as they arise. Regular assessments and adjustments ensure that the frameworks evolve with emerging threats and the organization's changing landscape.

By being proactive and emphasizing a comprehensive approach that includes both technological and human factors, organizations can create resilient security postures. Ultimately, the choice of framework is less about the framework itself and more about how well an organization commits to its implementation.

A practical tip is to begin with an organizational risk assessment. Understanding your unique environment and potential vulnerabilities can help tailor the chosen framework to fit better, ensuring that the security measures align with your specific needs and challenges.

13.2 Lessons Learned from Framework Failures

Analyzing cases where framework adoption has failed reveals important lessons. Many organizations embark on the journey to implement a cyber security framework, only to encounter significant roadblocks that inhibit progress. Common reasons for these failures often stem from inadequate understanding of the framework's requirements, lack of senior management support, and poor alignment with organizational goals. For instance, when a company adopted a well-regarded framework without tailoring it to their specific operational context, they faced compliance issues that ultimately strained resources and demotivated team members. The result was a fragmented approach to security that did not yield the anticipated benefits, illustrating that frameworks should not be seen as one-size-fits-all solutions. Expanding on this, many failures can be traced back to insufficient training and awareness amongst employees, leading to a culture where the framework is ignored or misunderstood. A clear takeaway from these instances is that the initial enthusiasm for framework adoption must be matched with education and resources to ensure a foundational understanding across all levels of the organization.

Discussing strategies to avoid similar pitfalls can provide valuable guidance for future implementations. Establishing strong leadership buy-in is critical; when management champions the framework, it fosters a culture of compliance and prioritizes security at an organizational level. Additionally, customizing the framework to fit the unique needs and risks of the organization can greatly enhance its effectiveness. This might involve engaging stakeholders from various departments to uncover their specific challenges and incorporating that feedback into the framework's application. Furthermore, investing in ongoing education and training ensures that every team member understands their role in maintaining the organization's security posture while using the framework. Regular review and adaptation of the implemented framework based on feedback and changing risks can also prevent stagnation and keep security measures relevant. Over time, this adaptive approach to framework implementation not only solidifies its integration into the organizational culture but actively contributes to building a mature cybersecurity ecosystem.

One practical tip for organizations is to initiate a pilot program before full-scale implementation of a framework. Engage a small team to apply the framework and document their experiences, challenges, and successes. This trial phase can surface potential issues early on and allow adjustments to be made based on real-world feedback before the full organization embarks on the framework journey. Such an approach not only reduces the risk of widespread failure but also fosters a sense of ownership and engagement from the outset, setting the stage for a successful framework adoption.

13.3 Emerging Trends and Future Outlook

Innovations in cyber security frameworks are becoming increasingly crucial as organizations strive to protect sensitive information against evolving threats. One significant trend is the adoption of adaptive security architecture, which allows cyber security measures to be more responsive to potential vulnerabilities. This approach employs automation and analytics to continually assess risks and adjust defenses in real-time, greatly enhancing an organization's resilience to cyber threats. Furthermore, frameworks that integrate cloud security are gaining traction as businesses migrate to cloud environments. As a result, frameworks like the NIST Cybersecurity Framework are evolving to include guidelines for securing cloud infrastructures, ensuring consistent protection irrespective of where information is stored or processed. The focus on zero trust architecture is another innovative practice emerging in the field; this principle assumes that threats could exist both outside and inside the network, prompting organizations to verify every request as if it originates from an untrusted source, which reinforces their security posture significantly.

Looking ahead, several projected trends may shape the future of cyber security frameworks. The rise of artificial intelligence and machine learning technologies is set to revolutionize threat detection and response. These technologies can analyze vast amounts of data at remarkable speeds, identifying patterns that could indicate impending cyber attacks more accurately than traditional methods. Moreover, regulatory changes are anticipated, with governments worldwide likely to impose stricter compliance requirements on organizations, particularly regarding data privacy and security standards. This will demand that existing frameworks adapt and evolve to align with these regulations. In addition, the continued expansion of the Internet of Things (IoT) means that cyber security frameworks will need to address the unique challenges posed by a broader and more diverse range of connected devices. Organizations will need to develop comprehensive strategies that encompass all devices in their ecosystems, thus ensuring robust security measures are in place.

To stay ahead of these emerging trends, professionals in the field must remain proactive in their approach. Engaging in continuous education and training will be essential, enabling cyber security experts to understand the latest technologies and integrate them into their security frameworks effectively. Joining professional organizations and attending industry conferences will foster collaboration and knowledge sharing, building a community that can better combat the complex landscape of cyber threats. Establishing a culture of security awareness within an organization can further enhance overall resilience, making cybersecurity an integral part of the organizational fabric rather than a checklist item. Monitoring these trends and adapting strategies accordingly can equip professionals to navigate the continually changing cyber security landscape successfully.

Chapter 14: Future Trends in Cyber Security Frameworks

14.1 Evolving Cyber Threat Landscape

The cyber threat landscape is constantly changing, shaped by technological advancements and the ever-evolving tactics of malicious actors. As new trends emerge, organizations must adapt their frameworks and strategies to effectively mitigate risks. Traditional security approaches often fall short against sophisticated threats such as ransomware, advanced persistent threats, and state-sponsored attacks. An adaptive cybersecurity framework emphasizes flexibility, enabling organizations to respond proactively rather than reactively. This flexibility allows for continuous monitoring, real-time threat intelligence integration, and swift adjustments to policies and practices. Implementing such a framework ensures defenders can effectively respond to emerging threats and vulnerabilities, which are often the result of increasingly interconnected systems and the rise of the Internet of Things (IoT).

Key threats that organizations should be particularly vigilant about include ransomware attacks, which have surged in recent years due to their ability to inflict immediate financial harm and operational disruption. Phishing attacks, which have grown more sophisticated, remain a primary vector for breaching defenses and gaining unauthorized access to sensitive data. Companies must also be aware of insider threats, whether intentional or accidental, as employees can unwittingly compromise organizational security. Furthermore, the increasing reliance on cloud-based services presents its own risks, with concerns surrounding data privacy and potential misconfigurations. Lastly, the rise of artificial intelligence not only aids defenders but also equips attackers with new tools, amplifying the landscape of potential risks.

Staying informed about these key threats and trends is essential for ensuring robust cybersecurity. Organizations should incorporate threat intelligence sharing into their frameworks, allowing them to learn from the experiences of others and adjust their defenses accordingly. Regular training and awareness programs can help cultivate a vigilant workforce that understands the evolving nature of threats. By fostering a culture of security, organizations can enhance their resilience against today's dynamic and increasingly complex cyber threat landscape.

14.2 Advances in Cyber Security Technologies

Technological advances have significantly transformed the cyber security landscape in recent years. Innovations such as artificial intelligence, machine learning, and automation have played pivotal roles in enhancing security measures. These technologies help in identifying and mitigating threats more efficiently by analyzing vast amounts of data in real-time. AI and machine learning, in particular, enable systems to learn from previous attacks and improve their defense mechanisms. This is crucial in a world where cyber threats are becoming increasingly sophisticated and frequent. Additionally, the rise of the Internet of Things (IoT) has expanded the attack surface, necessitating comprehensive security frameworks that can adapt to a myriad of connected devices. Effective endpoint detection and response (EDR) solutions have emerged, leveraging advanced analytics to provide organizations with improved insights into their security posture, allowing for earlier detection and remediation of potential breaches.

As organizations adopt cloud services, security measures are evolving to integrate seamlessly with cloud environments, fostering a more proactive approach to protecting sensitive data.

These advancements in technology will influence future frameworks and their development significantly. Cyber security frameworks will need to adapt to incorporate these emerging technologies while remaining relevant to the ever-evolving threat landscape. For instance, standards may emphasize the integration of AI in threat detection and response processes. As organizations increasingly rely on automated systems, there will be a greater focus on creating guidelines for ethical AI use in security, ensuring that algorithms are not only effective but also fair and transparent. Furthermore, frameworks will likely shift towards incorporating resilience and agility, allowing organizations to respond to incidents with minimal disruption. This emphasis on agility will require continuous updates and revisions to frameworks, as new threats emerge and technologies advance. Consequently, staying informed about the latest trends and engaging in ongoing professional development will be essential for security professionals aiming to implement these frameworks effectively.

To stay ahead in the ever-changing cyber security landscape, it is crucial for professionals to actively participate in forums and communities where the latest trends and innovations are discussed. Engaging with others in the field not only provides valuable insights but can also foster collaboration that leads to more robust security solutions.

14.3 Impact of Emerging Regulations

Emerging regulations are significantly reshaping cybersecurity practices on a global scale. Governments and regulatory bodies are recognizing the importance of protecting sensitive data against escalating cyber threats. This shift has led to the development of new laws that require organizations to adopt robust security measures. As regulations like the General Data Protection Regulation (GDPR) in Europe and the California Consumer Privacy Act (CCPA) become more prominent, businesses must reevaluate their cybersecurity frameworks to ensure compliance. These regulations often impose strict guidelines on data handling, privacy, and breach notification protocols, compelling organizations to adopt more comprehensive risk management strategies. Compliance not only protects organizations from potential fines but also enhances customer trust by demonstrating a commitment to data protection.

Despite the clear benefits, navigating these emerging regulations can present significant compliance challenges for many organizations. The complexity of different regulatory requirements can be daunting, especially for multinational companies that must align with varying laws across jurisdictions. Organizations often struggle to maintain compliance due to a lack of resources, insufficient staff training, and outdated technology systems. Furthermore, the pace of regulatory change means that cybersecurity frameworks must be continually updated to reflect new legal requirements. Companies may find themselves investing heavily in compliance solutions while balancing operational demands, leading to increased pressure on their cybersecurity budgets. It is critical for cybersecurity professionals to stay informed about the evolving regulatory landscape to identify gaps in their compliance strategies and address them proactively.

One practical approach to overcoming compliance challenges is to integrate regulatory requirements into existing cybersecurity frameworks. By adopting a risk-based approach that considers specific regulations, organizations can streamline their compliance efforts while enhancing overall security posture. Regular training and awareness programs for employees can also foster a culture of security and ensure that all staff understand their roles in compliance. Utilizing automation tools to monitor regulatory changes and compliance status can greatly reduce the manual burden on teams, allowing them to focus on strategic security initiatives instead of reactive compliance tasks. Leveraging these strategies will not only aid in meeting regulations but also position organizations for greater resilience in the face of cyber threats.

Chapter 15: Conclusion and Best Practices

15.1 Key Takeaways from Frameworks

Exploring various cybersecurity frameworks reveals critical insights that can enhance organizational resilience. One key takeaway is the importance of a structured approach to vulnerability management. Frameworks like NIST and ISO provide comprehensive guidelines that help organizations identify, assess, and mitigate risks systematically. This structured methodology not only promotes consistency but also ensures that all aspects of security, from technical controls to employee training, are carefully considered. Additionally, the emphasis on continuous improvement within these frameworks highlights the necessity for organizations to adapt to evolving threats and technologies. Regular assessments and updates of security measures foster a culture of vigilance and preparedness that is essential in today's dynamic cyber landscape.

Throughout the analysis of various frameworks, several overarching themes emerge that reinforce the critical components of effective cybersecurity practices. First, collaboration and communication across departments are emphasized consistently. Silos can obstruct risk management efforts, making integrated security efforts across the organization vital. Furthermore, the alignment between business objectives and cybersecurity initiatives is a recurring theme, illustrating how security should be viewed as a business enabler rather than a hindrance. Lastly, the focus on governance and compliance underscores the relevance of maintaining accountability and transparency in cybersecurity efforts. By adhering to established standards and frameworks, organizations can not only safeguard their assets but also demonstrate credibility and responsibility to stakeholders.

Understanding these insights from cybersecurity frameworks can significantly affect how a professional approaches security in their organization. Practicing regular reviews and updates of security protocols based on framework recommendations can lead to a more dynamic and responsive security posture, ensuring organizations are not just reacting to threats but proactively managing them. Consider establishing a routine that involves cross-departmental meetings to facilitate communication and gather diverse perspectives on security challenges. This practice not only enhances the effectiveness of your security strategy but also fosters a culture of shared responsibility for protecting organizational assets.

15.2 Strategies for Effective Implementation

Organizations aiming to implement cybersecurity frameworks effectively must start by establishing a solid foundation that includes a comprehensive understanding of the specific framework they intend to adopt. It is crucial to customize the framework to align with the organization's unique needs, culture, and risk landscape. This involves conducting a thorough risk assessment to identify vulnerabilities and prioritize security measures accordingly. To ensure successful execution, organizations should create a detailed implementation plan that outlines specific roles, responsibilities, and timelines. Engaging stakeholders early in the process can facilitate smoother collaboration and buy-in, which is essential for fostering a culture of security. Additionally, leveraging technology can enhance implementation efforts; tools that automate compliance reporting and monitoring can greatly reduce manual effort and human error, thus streamlining the overall approach to compliance with the framework. Consistent communication across all levels of the organization during this process ensures that everyone is informed and aware of their responsibilities in maintaining the security posture.

Training and engagement play a pivotal role in the successful implementation of cybersecurity frameworks. A well-informed workforce is one of the first lines of defense against cyber threats. Organizations should prioritize regular training and awareness programs that not only educate employees about the framework but also emphasize the importance of their individual roles in maintaining security. Hands-on training allows employees to apply their knowledge in realistic scenarios, fostering confidence and competence. Moreover, creating an ongoing feedback loop where employees can share their insights and suggestions can significantly enhance engagement and adherence to security protocols. Involving employees in the development of security policies and practices ensures that the framework resonates with them, leading to greater acceptance and proactive behavior regarding cybersecurity practices. Continuous engagement through refresher courses and awareness campaigns can help keep the security mindset alive within the organization, making it easier to adapt to evolving cyber threats.

Effective implementation is not a one-time event but an ongoing process. Organizations should regularly review and refine their strategies based on evolving threats and emerging technologies. Creating a culture of continuous improvement, where feedback is valued and adaptations are made swiftly, can significantly contribute to the robustness of the cybersecurity framework in place. Understanding that cybersecurity is a shared responsibility encourages collaboration and a collective commitment to maintaining security. As a practical tip, organizations may benefit from conducting regular internal audits and penetration testing exercises to evaluate the effectiveness of their implementation and uncover areas for improvement.

15.3 Building a Culture of Cyber Security

Fostering a culture of security within organizations is crucial in today's digital landscape. It goes beyond simply implementing security protocols; it involves nurturing an environment where every employee understands their role in safeguarding sensitive information. When security is ingrained in the very fabric of an organization's culture, it becomes second nature for employees to prioritize cybersecurity in their daily tasks. Such a culture empowers staff to identify potential risks and respond proactively, creating a collective sense of responsibility. This shared commitment to security not only protects assets but also enhances organizational resilience against cyber threats. Organizations that cultivate this culture typically experience fewer security incidents, as employees are more vigilant and informed when it comes to recognizing suspicious activities or behavior.

Engaging all levels of staff in security awareness is essential for establishing a robust security culture. It starts with clear communication about the importance of cybersecurity and how every individual plays a part in the organization's defense strategy. Best practices for achieving widespread engagement include organizing regular training sessions that make cybersecurity concepts relatable and actionable. These sessions should encourage employees to ask questions, share their concerns, and discuss real-world scenarios that highlight potential threats. Incorporating gamification elements into training can also increase participation and retention of information. Furthermore, seeking input from employees on security policies acknowledges their perspective and fosters a sense of ownership over security practices. Recognizing and rewarding employees who actively contribute to security initiatives further motivates the workforce to stay vigilant and engaged.

As organizations strive to build a culture of cybersecurity, they should remember that continuous improvement is key. Regularly assessing the effectiveness of security initiatives and soliciting feedback from staff can reveal areas for enhancement. Additionally, leveraging security champions within teams can promote consistent messaging and support across departments. These champions serve as liaisons who educate peers, reinforcing the idea that cybersecurity is everyone's responsibility. A proactive approach that keeps security dialogues ongoing will not only enhance awareness but also adapt to emerging threats. One practical tip for fostering a culture of security is to ensure that cybersecurity is included in everyday conversations, making it a regular topic in meetings and discussions. This approach embeds security awareness into the organizational ethos, helping everyone recognize its importance in achieving the overall success of the organization.